Mindfullessons

Mindfullessons

The Journey into the Heart and Mind

By

Therapeutic Speaker:

Christopher Cole

Note: Please read! Behind these pages lay the commonsense secrets to unlocking your greatest potential. Start living the life you want today, financially, physically and emotionally. Living a fulfilled life is simple it just requires for you to not be afraid of the simplicity before you.

To my Mother –

The angel behind the man.

Section I

Preface

Longfellow once said "Success is doing what you can do well and doing well whatever you do."

Confucius says "Wherever you go, go with all of your heart."

When I was young I wanted to become a Neuro-Ophthalmologist, reflecting today, I can understand more what attracted me to that field. Looking back, I would like to think now that my life's calling was just as powerful as the Demigod Hercules; it was the calling to bring sight to the sight-less and help restore vision to those who have shut their eyes in fear and desperation. Restoring vision to purpose and potential is the primary calling of Mindfullessons. With it I hope to help the world restore itself one person at a time.

To understand me more I will tell you that
I was reared in a single mother household but
as Yoda might say I lacked not.
Why is this?
Well as Kai Greene has said "There was never
a night or a problem that could defeat sunrise."
That quote illustrates
This revolutionary "hope" I felt in my life
It propelled me into a consciousness of lacking
not,

*a mindset of complete gratitude and openness
to new things.
As the Rock says "If something stands
between you and your success move it
Never be denied"
That fit perfectly with what
Mom taught me "No is not in your vocabulary"
She was right.
So I stand here,
A Certain Man
Designed for a Certain Mission
To help serve as a "Man for Others"*

I've lived a journey. What I learned from life is that if you waste time, time will waste you. This however isn't meant to scare you. It is to encourage you to listen more carefully to your inner calling.

Thank You

I owe much respect to all of those righteous souls who stood to teach, mentor, and love me. Whether you knew it or not you were helping to change the world. I will never forget the generosity shown to me. From the doors opened to the right doors closed thank you for caring enough to see my passage to manhood be one that even the stars could rejoice in. As Mahatma Gandhi once said "Be the change you want to see in the world." I'm doing just that, and you my friends have done the same. Those who read this book, remember, helping a child can be one of the most powerfully rewarding things you can do. If in your power, leave no one within your reach hungry, or sad. Give them the wisdom to quench the thirst within the mind, and the words to satisfy the soul and the love of God to comfort their being.

Stop Holding Back and Waiting

There comes a time when you have to commit yourself and your actions all in before you can begin to see the results you want in your life. Too often people manage to build a false reality of why they should wait to take action-Things like "I should wait until I am better at it, or until the world ask me to do it."- But in reality the gift comes during the process of refining your actions with doing. We must understand that it is time for us to do and no longer to wait for the right moment to start making it happen. We cannot let the fear of failure prevent us from hyper performing and giving all of ourselves now. That's like a basketball team waiting to train hard until they know they are going to win the championship. To achieve great things one must first believe they can win, then agree that they are achieving it, be happy they are going to win and then continue to work like they would work with having achieved the victory.

Running on Empty

How can one be satisfied if empty and lost? Unable to command ones day, not able to defend against distraction and opposition. From having traveled the world from China to India I have found practices which lead me back to the same foundations you find in Christianity. It is the call to ground one's self, and move with clarity for achieving development over one's life. A person who does not develop their life ceases to experience the substantial feelings of progress and refinement. It is clear that with stagnation comes depression and the feeling of not being able to achieve anything. With time these negative emotions can serve to cloud the better person within. However, if you want to change your life then you need to begin interacting with your daily endeavors and seeking to have more command over your life experience. This power will enable you to turn negative experiences into positive experiences and when you do this, then your world opens up an atmosphere of infinite possibility. I have studied leading experts in the area of personal achievement and with that mixed in my immense passion for spiritual practice. The product is that of understanding how to gain deep spiritual balance and extraordinary freedom in one's life, financially, physically, and emotionally. The secret is that it starts with your thinking and believing, and in time through conscious refinement, perfection begins to appear.

The talents of a Man

"Surrender is essentially an operation by means of which we set about explaining instead of acting."
- Charles Peguy

Crisp with focus upon all who stand around you, perched within a subjective mind and uncertain body you stand confronted to act. Your mind trembles with voluminous concerns as to how to be right, how to select the right path and how to muster all of your strength to act. Just do it as they say, really hiding the words "do it right the first time or fall to criticism and failure" these are the very thoughts many people have when disempowering themselves; this is the challenge of a person who acts. @Manforothers

Life does not have to end each day with the sorrow that befalls from thinking in a way that apprehends one from productive living. It should instead be capacious with infinite possibility. How can you cultivate this type of living? Well, it starts with how you perceive things. Life is all about perception and what you believe to be a reality for yourself. Your life is limited by how far you can dream. The distance between success and failure is how far you are willing to go which is purely controlled by your thoughts. If you know that you are going to meet criticism with positive thoughts and comments than you will train yourself to release negative things to spare yourself the pain that's holding you back. If you vow only to accept excellence, thus surrounding yourself with it from the food you eat to the people you linger with to the things you allow into your mind then will begin to produce excellence in your life. Thinking you want more is not as convincing as thinking and then acting to produce more for yourself. Your life changes with the action you take. Let's consider the B.J. Fogg Behavior Model which examines how you go from no action to action. The B.J Fogg behavior model represents the formula B=MAT what these variables stand for in essence is that there are three things which work to stimulate action, those things are: Sufficient motivation for doing the action, ease of ability to complete the action, and a trigger to begin the behavior. So in order to move towards action one must focus on producing enough emotional power to get them to a state of wanting to take action, then eliminate all limiting excuses and begin creating positive actions feelings towards doing what needs to be done.

Begin with only allowing yourself to share with others, positive things. Stop judging that which is not yours to judge and take a strong hold over the things you focus on. Like Confucius says: "If we fail to see the righteousness in others we ourselves are lack of righteousness." Confucius defines righteousness as being when good is mixed not only with action but the contemplated intent to do good in ones endeavors. This means having a harness over your thoughts and actions but not felling defeated if you mess up or make mistakes on your journey.

Why

"Why" is a common question asked of God and the Universe. But how powerful could it be if people started instead to say wow, thank God that was me. I am glad I slipped on that patch of ice and caught myself, now I know to walk a different way next time.

Figuring Life Out

*"It's not our differences that separate us,
but instead our inability to work together in
equality and understanding." – @Manforothers*

I am calling attention to people's nature to not
want to accept another's short comings, or societal
defined failure. This is a huge loss for human
relationship. Without mistakes there can be no
greatness, therefore the excuse that others are
wrong is really a bold acceptance of ones non-
willingness to attentively listen to other people, or
even genuinely look within. Those who truly are
the most happy and successful people in this world
can do these things and can appreciate everything
from a babies cry to an old person's wise mumble.
There is value in emissions from the heart, it is
called sincerity. If you open your eyes and look pass
racial, sexual, or economic identities you can begin
to see people.

Yoga of truth

"Those who achieve great things understand that when trying to achieve something there is no such thing as failure only recorded ways of how to not do something."-@Manforothers

Sri T once said that "Yoga is the process of building new more appropriate habits". Habits are the foundations for the results we build in our lives. From financial freedom to living stress free, it is done by being in control of your life through harnessing the power of each day. If you want to achieve it then believe you are the person you need to be to have it and with time you will do the things you need to do to become that person. Directions come from within, that guidance is called grace by some, the universal mindset by others, but the truth remains this power rest within all who "breathe".

Cruise Control

"Boxing champions breathe like boxing champions. If you want to be a boxing champion you have to first breathe like one." –@Manforothers

Control does not mean getting what you want upfront, control means being able to endure any situation and still walk away with something that can catalyze growth in your life. If you learn how to have appreciation for things as simple as the breath, you can then begin to use it to your advantage.

If you can tolerate the process of finding purpose and serenity then you can allow others naturally to share with you things that can help you knowingly or unknowingly. What they share can be used in building your ship. Don't forget those who usually have the most to add, still allow others to shine, as they can find even more beauty in learning and sharing experience. This ability to stay calm and grounded in the present, turns into power as you can see clearly what you want, and notice when you aren't getting it. That connection with your life is so powerful it can allow you to shape and re-shape your actions, relationships and even identity to match with the future you are envisioning. This is the power of fulfilling your destiny.

Release the Raft

Being continually stressed out is caused most often by the habits we have for how we view situations and things that happen to us. Psychologist have shown us that individuals who deal with guilt are most often doomed to repeat the action causing affliction in one's life.

Just thinking about something and then waiting is not the key to building a stress free life. It takes much more than--- contemplating your master plan--- but it requires your total commitment and willingness to follow your inner voice and grace towards taking new actions and releasing the old.

 When I get a great inspiration or idea, I write it down, and then immediately, take the necessary action to bring it about. The journey does not stop there, it continues for how long you choose to take it, and as long as you can feel in your inner heart that you are supposed to be doing something about it. In order to get to a new place in life it requires that you build the right raft. The directions for this raft however don't come purely from research alone, directions often come from within. If you give up on the first try then you'll never build the right raft or get to your new destination. This however is not meant to compel you to work harder in your own effort but instead to relax more and become more obedient to the things you should be doing. For me I place my faith in the reality that God has already made possible for me the thing I am seeking to achieve, therefore I have gratitude for my ability to rest in knowing it has already been done, and that I can rely on my inner calmness and directional force.

Like many things in life you can easily be imprisoned by actions, thoughts, and feelings that in the end are more than toxic but detrimental to your healthy existence, so stop now being so worried or condemned, there is no condemnation with God, and certainly there should be none with you.

Doubt No More

"Life isn't always about setting goals but life definitely is about having clarity and purpose."
-@Manforothers

I cannot stress enough how important it is to have purpose for the things you do in life. You need to have purpose or you can easily begin to live the life other people want you to live and not the one you are designed to live. Have you ever gotten up to go to work and felt like you were hitting a dead-end in the road? That's because you have no fulfillment, and at the very least you cannot see the good in what you are doing, or even a goal you are working toward.

Seeking fulfillment may sound simple to do but can also become a burden of stress if you let it and don't stick to your goals. You may find yourself jumping around from new idea to the next, and allowing yourself some cheat days, and maybe even time off. Not achieving the goals you are expecting to see immediately can create huge levels of doubt that can grow so large they make you want to give up, become depressed, and do nothing. Do not allow this to happen! That cycle can become a pattern in your life if you let it. It's like taking your eyes off the prize as soon as you are about to grab it and missing it and getting angry each time. So stop doing the things that cause you to lose momentum and refocus on the things you want. Empower yourself each day, with action and emotional intensity behind your visions and the things you know you need to do to make your dreams a reality.

Breakout Plan

Ever found yourself staring at the computer doubting yourself, your dreams and your purpose? Sure it happens to the best of us, but I have learned that to break out of that daunting cloud of sadness and paralysis get up and act, do one thing that you have to do, and get it done, then do the next. I call it the break out plan. It's very overwhelming when you have so much to do, that you can't seem to do anything. So try beginning a project you have been putting off. After doing at least one thing, you will feel empowered and back on track. Many people also fear there isn't enough time, so it's critical that they do the most important thing, yet often end up doing nothing. When choosing what to do, select the thing which benefits you the most at the moment. Which task if completed can bring immediate satisfaction to you emotionally, spiritually, or physically? Researchers have found that we are most effective when we set time limits according to need of action. So don't let things consume all your time and keep it movin!

Stop Sitting There Just Thinking

Start working and creating, Move! If you continually try to organize and figure things out before you begin, you end up not doing much at all. Either you figured out why it wouldn't work – gee thanks- or you have overwhelmed yourself once again to the point of feeling too bogged down to take any action. Like Guy Kawasaki taught in his start up book, "fix it, then ship it" don't' fix it, fix it and fix it! Get out there and start doing things, then you will figure out what needs to be figured out. With time if you learn to listen to your inner guide, your plan of action for achieving success will become clear.

Share your Greatness with the World

Some people look blankly into the world thinking "If others only knew how smart I am or what beautiful things I have to offer, then I would be _____" I call those the dreamers with no action to back it up. Don't be the person who lives in no-man's land filled with deep levels of disappointment. Instead, share with the world your art. If you have something to offer that can help others, don't wait for your moment to shine, go out there and start living it. Doing this helps add strength to your purpose. Appreciate every moment of failure; because hey you tried, even when the world doubted your ability!

Breaking the Cycle of Uncertainty

I've battled most of my life with these thoughts: Am I doing what I am supposed to do? What about my visions for my future, hell what about the so called meaning of my future? It doesn't seem I am living like I am supposed to. I'm tired of being fat with no money. But, I want to do God's will so I will stay focused. I am sure a lot of people have had similar thoughts. The solution to breaking this ritualistic patter of disempowering yourself is to empower yourself which you can begin doing today by setting new patterns. You can't get many places worth getting to without any energy. It takes power and power is everything. The way you empower yourself is simple, yet requires persistence and a change of life. You can't keep doing the same things and expecting different results; Shakespeare defined that as insanity. You must create a list of possible places you want to go, and things you want to achieve. If you can't see yourself making it to those places you need to start with strengthening your visualization of your future. Once you can visualize it, you can make it a reality. In time you will become more comfortable with the richer things in your future and work to progressively build that powerful future.

When you Build

When building anything from an App to writing a book, build in the simplest arena. Trying to write a book in the format you will have it published can slow you down, same with building an app. Sometimes people get caught up on the design over function and forget that they could simply go through the wire framing stage. A great computer interface designer and consultant once shared with me that the best way to figure out if the crap works or not is to have it tested by people using the wire framing version. This makes the tester think the app is nowhere near completion. This mindset allows the person to become more judgmental instead of looking at a 70% finished product and being told to find out what's wrong, the person in this situation would most likely just want to change a few colors and not really get to the functionality. So the core of creation and best creations focus much attention upon the root and foundation. Everything from erecting world renowned buildings to self-cultivation requires you weed out the destructive parts early on and focus on the foundation. From parenting to personal development, if you allow bad things to linger, like weeds they can grow to take over the entire garden.

You can have it your way

Why build or create in a place you don't want to? Make things work for you, forever and always. Like my mother would always say, "Don't work harder but smarter". Think of what you want to accomplish, and then go for it but recognize how you do it. Ask yourself the right questions, like "Am I doing this the most efficient way?" Is the direction I'm headed really the one that will bring me the most fulfillment? How is what I am doing or going to do add value to myself or my mission to succeed? Asking the right questions can reveal a lot. If you can focus with emotional intensity on the things you want -as though you already had them- then your mind will begin to make it real. That realness will help support your decision making.

There's Room for One More, ok Maybe Two

I want you right now to crush those limiting thoughts you get about your new ideas and passions like – "that there is no room for me" or "someone else is already doing it"- So, do it better! There are a host of examples of following your dreams no matter what. Do you think LeBron James should have said "Well, Michael Jordon is already the best so why even try?" No! Of course not, instead LeBron James had a dream and went for it, and with his immense effort the universe made a space for him. When in doubt, think of all the gas stations, dating sites, and restaurants that are successful. Going for it may show you that the thing you thought you wanted wasn't the right thing anyway, which often leads to reveling what you were meant to have to begin with. I believe that with God's help and the Universe of infinite power there will be a special place for you to grow and become successful. The game is always changing. You never know you might be the next person to change the game. So go for it!

Control the Fear Scale

A student procrastinates writing a paper in the beginning because they fear of the challenge. Then at the last moment they get empowered to do it because the fear of not doing, ridicule and failure that comes along with it, outweighs the fear of doing. Learning to control the scale of fear within your own mind can mean the difference in achieving and not.

Speak it to See it

Determining something to be your purpose or goal isn't merely enough, each morning within the hour you wake, reinforce the ideas goals dreams and aspirations by going through them verbally while moving and breathing and thanking God for blessing you with it. Your brain will with each day activate to begin to connect the dots, you will also begin to receive advice more clearly which can help direct you. All the faith you build with verbal acceptance is the path your manifestation will take to deliver your desires into your life.

Go from mumbling through life to loud thanksgiving.

Stop Mumbling Through Life

Not planning your goals and just working for the hell of it, is like being half asleep and mumbling , you feel like you are saying something but you really aren't saying anything. With no clarity or commitment to your purpose, you mumble through life. A goal may be in your head but without direct action or explanation it stays there and really does not get you the results you desire. How do you combat this? Well it's not merely by planning or marking a calendar, it is by day in and day out living in a mindset of accomplishment for your specific request. Knowing God has already given it to you and made a way for you, is everything.

The biggest reason why people don't change their lives is because they think it is too late, but it only takes one second to banish that thought and visualize yourself turning around for good. Therefore it is never too late.

The Set Up

Give yourself positive reinforcement, don't narrowly expect it from others. You have to train yourself to visualize what you want but then reinforce those images and feelings with actions and words. I like to puff up my chest and suck in my gut and like a King proclaiming from a tower, I proclaim all the amazing things I will achieve, and consider all the beautiful things I have been given: like running water and sunlight, oh yea and trees!

People Fall Everyday

"Our greatest glory is not in never failing, but in rising up every time we fail."

"Our chief want is someone who will inspire us to be what we know we could be."

— Ralph Waldo Emerson

People fall every day from roadblocks, depressions, let downs, and personal failures. There is always time for you to focus on the failure in your life. But if you are so busy focusing on your failure you cannot embrace your successes. What happens to a child if you ignore them until they grow up? You get a child who often turns into a hurt grownup who lacks respect for older people. They have no reason for love, and often find it difficult to associate any positivity to life. If you ignore your incremental growth over time in reaching your goals, because you can't see the end result right away, then you are missing the point of life, which is to embrace the struggle. You must see the struggle as the fire which forges the sword. Most of all you must appreciate your development. Just as all children deserved to be loved and cultivated by everyone along the way so too should your small achievements.

A Mind Lost in Hell

The art is never to let One's mind linger;

Hell on earth is when you are unhealthy:

Unhealthy is when you are unable to become that which you were meant to be. This is the root of a miserable existence.

How can we escape hell on earth?

Find peace in all that you do. Find peace in your decision to do it, and take back control of your thoughts and actions.

As I said before: "If it does not go through the heart before the mind it is not divine." I wanted to convey the importance of following your thought and heart. Confucius taught that a cultivated man understands his ways, not because he is naturally wise but because he is cultivating himself. Cultivation comes from the toil, refinement, and struggle in taking note of one's daily doings and subjecting themself to the scrutiny of distillation. Questions one may ask is, "Am I following a righteous path?" Did I commit to actions which resulted in increased positive change in my life, or did I fall victim to my erosive thoughts? When a person can do this daily then they can truly work on being a righteous person with piety.

Exit Strategy

In those territories of doom always understand your exit strategy for having clarity of mind. If you learn what is causing you to fall, you can gradually cut it out. If it's a way of thinking that is leaving you underpowered and leading you towards misery, you can quickly change it if you simply focus on something else, like your goals, when a destructive thought creeps in. You must learn to re-empower yourself. No great garden is permanent by itself, it requires a gardener who guards it with a careful eye.

Omnificent

You can do anything as long as you don't hide from the things you know you should be doing. That clarity and peace comes from following what you understand in your heart and mind to be right. You can't always know if you are going to be right, but you can always understand your narrative and inspiration for the things you do. To make any real change you must first start understanding how to listen to your first mind, inner voice, and God's direction. When you learn how to silence your flesh and follow your spirit your regrets will fall behind because not only are you confidently making decisions, you are in fact the one making them, thus empowering your ability to have control over your life.

Sacrifice

People say "But WHY do I have to forgive? I sacrifice all the time". That may be true but the secret to breaking sadness and emotional penalization happens when you mentally forgive others. That forgiveness may not make you adore the person but it does allow you to move forward with your life. The hurt may always be there, but instead of looking at it as destructive begin to recognize it as the contributing force that makes your character stronger.

How to break through pain.

We wait for a person or thing to take us to the next level but the truth is, it happens only through our own realizations and growth. That person or thing just helps us along our way.

Breathe Your Way to Success

Breath brings Prana, which is life force. If you have life force you can do great things.

If you learn how to control your breath you control the life force, if you control your life force, you can control your whole attitude, actions, reactions, and thoughts, making you more powerfully able to achieve greatness.

Understanding the breath can offer you many things. Learning how to recognize the breath, helps you to develop a respect for it. If everything we are is essentially biochemistry, then the breath is more complicated than we think because it serves as a signal to both our inner and outer world. It can signal change in your outer world just as it can conduct change on your inner world. From your attitude to actions and health. The breath was at the beginning of it all.

Potential Greater than Outer Space

"The journey to the moon starts with the flip of a switch." @Manforothers

Strategies I use to understanding what it is I am supposed to do

1.   I determine if being successful at it requires me to change my current state and situation. If it requires me to make positive developmental change, will it bring me more joy and success than expected in the first place?

2.   Define what it is I want in life. Be courageous and dream up situations that may seem virtually impossible but could be done in a movie situation without looking too fake. Meaning I can achieve the impossible just make sure it is something that is obtainable materialistically, even if it has to be invented.

3.   Consider my surroundings, how will society look around me when I achieve these things. Will I be distant so far that everyone could disappear and I wouldn't care or would my success be something other people could look to for encouragement?

Make Yourself and Your Mission Special

Who likes to lose things special to them? Not many people, so make your mission so renowned in your mind that even if others do not understand it, you can count on it becoming a reality showing people, you are in fact different and you are special. When you do this you begin committing yourself to living your life in an extraordinary way. You can start holding yourself to a higher standard and finding justification for going the extra mile and moving with purpose. Doing this equips you with clarity of purpose.

See Good

Take the opportunity when handed to you. Start learning how to grow from your life experiences. Everyday things are handed to us through experiences, so with each moment if your mind is within the state of positive energy you will be emitting a signal of attraction for more positive things to come to you. The purpose of living in a mindset of gratitude is to be able to make use of all the wonderful things we have access to everyday.

In this thinking the phrase goes "Try to see the good in everything."

Daily Actions

There seems to be this huge gap in everything we do, we are either doing something that is working, or doing nothing which always gets you no results. I call it working with no results. Humans hate having no progress to account for the hard work they invest into their physical or financial life. This fear is what often grows into a person's refusal to imagine more. So in order to move forward you must understand how to do the smallest things and find appreciation for them. This will take pressure away from your mind whether you achieved anything or not. As I stated earlier in this book, "in order to get the ball rolling and push past a paralyzing state you need to do one thing that's in your power to do at that moment."

Track Life

Success comes in life when you get around the right people and right things. You can run as fast as you want, but you will never compete with the top runners if you are not on the same track. Your efforts will be to no avail if you don't first look, learn, and understand how to get your life on the right track. Right track is everything: from the right thinking, to the right people, actions, habits and environment.

Know your Health Know your Dharma

You will know what you are supposed to be doing if you can: Envision your happiness and success while doing (what your idea of action) is and then see yourself asking the world "why the hell did you not tell me to do it earlier?"… "You mean to tell me, you were going to allow me to miss my calling?"

I realized that when I pictured myself living out the reality I wanted, I felt certainly it was the one I knew I should be living. With this self-encouragement, nothing could, can, or will stop me.

Section 2 II "Quote Me"

A higher calling has already been determined to work for you because it comes from a higher vision that can see what you cannot. - Christopher Cole

When in question, now is always better than later. Later doesn't exist it is created or experienced. - Christopher Cole

The battle of life is all about being able to understand yourself enough to know what is for you and what is not. – Christopher Cole

Boxing champions breathe like boxing champions. If you want to be a boxing champion you have to first breathe like one. –Christopher Cole

God has your greatest life/ potential written, it is your choice to take it. - Christopher Cole

"The hardest place in life is where you give just enough not to give up but not enough to live fully in who you are meant to be." - Christopher Cole

"Don't be like the bird free falling and not knowing when to flap its wings." - Christopher Cole

"The goal in life should be not to struggle to reject the flesh, but instead cultivate enough through daily refinement that you won't have to." – Christopher Cole

"You stay condemned only for how long you replay, recycle your pain. There is no condemnation with God, only grace." @Manforothers

"Living fast and full of your passion potential is different than living a life of reaction."   - Christopher Cole

"Allow yourself to make decisions without regret. Learn how to reflect over a day's passage. From it you learn what's best for you." - Christopher Cole

"Your stability is everything, gain a deeper faith, and have faith more often in the things you can't see. This way you can achieve anything great! " - Christopher Cole

"A belief in God will strengthen your belief in yourself to have the power to change the world around you." - Christopher Cole

"People don't want to help others because they think they must then neglect themselves. This is not true. Every living human has the opportunity to be a blessing. As the saying goes "I am blessed to be a blessing." - Christopher Cole

"You are not living your dream by living in a dream." - Christopher Cole

"Stop questioning what to do, instead embrace your life story as preparation enough for the task ahead of you." - Christopher Cole

"You have to expect more, then do more, to get more." - Christopher Cole

"Successful people don't give up in fear of hard times but persist knowing and trusting in their ability to survive and pull through." - Christopher Cole

"You don't always do from knowing how. You figure out a way by doing without knowing how and eureka before you know it, it is clear what to do. The point is to have faith and live life with reflection, everything is impossible until you do it." - Christopher Cole

"Uncertainty is the veil of the enemy and discouragement is the spear." - Christopher Cole

"It's Important to focus on the intensity level of your thoughts. This intensity can be the power which helps you create new, more appropriate thoughts or fall to less appropriate ones." - Christopher Cole

"You can change your life in an instant or live normal for a whole life time." - Christopher Cole

"Be the answer to your future you are waiting for today!" - Christopher Cole

"Things are very connected. Sometimes we choose to ignore the connection in hopes we can make excuses for our failures. Stop visualizing and expecting failure. Instead begin believing in your success." - Christopher Cole

"You can't always reason your way out of bed. But you can always empower yourself to want more and pull yourself out of bed to go get it." - Christopher Cole

"Not knowing where you stand in life is just as dangerous as standing in the wrong place." -Christopher Cole

"Don't make your method a necessity make your will to achieve and create your future a necessity." ------Christopher Cole

"An unrealistic schedule results in achieving unrealistic goals. Yet when you begin to see your schedule as achievable you can see your dreams as obtainable." - Christopher Cole

"Do you quietly ask for more or speak out with gratitude for what you know you already have." - Christopher Cole

"Sometimes you have to close your eyes to begin to see." - Christopher Cole

"Spend 100% percent of your time on solutions and not problems." - Christopher Cole

"To change your life, the Universe only asks a little bit from you and that is to change your belief system, and exhibit a little bit more discipline." - Christopher Cole

"Thinking alone does not unlock your universe, instead, speaking, chanting, and moving does. When is a Christian Church service most emotionally moving? When people are praising and dancing."   - Christopher Cole

"Don't let the stress of not doing overwhelm the stress of doing." - Christopher Cole

"God will call the spirit will choose to answer." - Christopher Cole

"Saying what your plan is going to be for success is not as powerful as acting and then seeing what your plan should be." - Christopher Cole

"The art of war for life is called: the art of follow through." - Christopher Cole

"There is a thin line between success and not success, the same thin line between doing and not doing. Action is the core of success." - Christopher Cole

"Wealth, honor, blessing, and benefit are meant for the enrichment of my life, while poverty, humble station, care, and sorrow will be my helpmates to fulfillment." - Dr. Keenan

"Greatness only takes one night to manifest; at a time." - Christopher Cole

"Sometimes when you stumble upon responsibility, God is giving you a gift (Rather than a burden) and you don't even know it." - Christopher Cole

"Flowers make the most beautiful scent s when they are crushed." - Christopher Cole

"Sometimes, we need the outside to remind us to have inner peace" - Christopher Cole

"The only difference between intelligent design and randomness is discipline" - Christopher Cole

"The woman you have confidence to speak to may not be the woman of your dreams" - Christopher Cole

"People are always lacking somewhere, so never envy. And those who are fulfilled, take note" - Christopher Cole

"If you train your focus like you would train a dragon, you will be able to direct your fire wherever you want it to go." - Christopher Cole

"There are many vehicles one can take to get to their destination, no matter the vehicle you are always going to hit some potholes."- Christopher Cole

Mindfullessons from India

The Yoga of Truth- what you will read here is a vanity of what I learned and conceived while in India studying Yoga under the guidance of Ravi Shankar.

"Life is not merely about setting goals and achieving them, life is about growing, experiencing new things while helping other people."
@Manforothers

Those who achieve great things know that when trying to achieve something there is no such thing as failure, only recorded ways of how not to do something. If you want to achieve it then believe you are the person you need to be to have it.

The foundation of an enjoyed existence is one that feels it is doing what it is meant to be doing. In order to influence these feelings within yourself, you have to actively play a role in commanding your circumstance in life. With time after time you command the life you want to live in, you will effortlessly begin to do the right thing. So first learn who you are.

"The practice of Yoga helps you to focus on the essentials of your being."

How Yoga can save your life

You must learn how to both give and still focus on your own development.

Some give more than others, and sometimes it is not your obligation to give. However, we all gain a chance to share something with someone, and when you share you begin to see what tremendous value you are to the world. This feeling is one that can help you to achieve a motivated state of achieving more.

Fear

When you begin to realize that you are your safety net, and that God is holding your net tight, then there is nothing to fear.

Moving past fear is the first step towards walking the journey into stability. Learning how to disprove your fear is a matter of understanding what drives you and ignoring what stops you. Whether it be personal actions or contemplation of venomous words from others you need to be the operator of your progression. In life things are driven by our creativity and ability to see it through. It is true that God opens doors for us, but it's no use if we aren't walking through them; what good would it be to open a door for someone only so that they could stand there and not walk through?

Why Mindfulness Is So Important According to the teaching of Yoga:

"There is a point where two things meet, everything going on in the world around us is in constant transition from one moment to the next."

Through practice of mindfulness one with time can learn how to be aware when things are making transition. Even with the passing of night to day the sun changes to night (while moving)

I have begun to see things as being the reality that grounding ourselves is one step, the next comes the ability to sacrifice through doing a practice and refinement. This turns into a recycling process.

Through doing this, you begin to see that all things are connected.

One Being to a Whole

There is a concept in Yoga of everything functioning as one. One function works to serve the other function and both serve the whole. This belief is powerful in being able to help uncover your role in life. Purely it is important to cultivate yourself as you fit into the whole universal existence. If you suffer from a mindset of "lack" then that will contribute to how you treat others.

"Everything functions as one. All parts of the body are doing what they must, but for a greater plan. It's all connected it's called the Vadanta."
Remember a janitor is just as important as the medical doctors who are in a hospital all function to complete the whole.

Opening up Happiness

Yoga was created to release you from your sorrow.

Being unhealthy means much more than the pounds, it means being bound, lost, and unable to take control of your life's full potential! This truth led me to feverously seek wisdom and knowledge from sources that taught real strategies I could use to erase the feeling of being stuck and open my vision to seeing the bright light down the road.

In India I learned that the quality of life force is unbounded happiness also called Unanda or Bliss.

Lasting relief, bliss and joy is the ability to accept with happiness what is already happening. It is the ability to ignore negativity and build upon opportunity to actively make sure limiting actions are removed catalyzing the stopping of negative states of mind.

6 Enemies of the Mind

In order the 6 enemies of the mind are: Desire, Intoxication (mental captivity, drugs, beauty…) Anger, Arrogance (pride) Greed and Envy. These enemies are not meant to be dwelled upon, instead I listed them to help illustrate areas to consider when working to becoming healthy. If you are tired of your current life circumstance you must first believe yourself to be in a new life circle then actively determine which enemy is holding you back from stable growth.

Winning Clarity of Mind

I believe you have it in you, however, it is up to you to make your mind up.

Below are steps Yoga teaches on how to open up clarity. So to begin to tap into your full potential, it is noted that you have to work within your bounds of understanding. Before building a new home, you must first envision it to begin the blueprint, which will then lead to the actions to make it a reality.

So if you are finding yourself hitting a mental roadblock practice building clarity.

Steps to unleashing Clarity:

1.   What's holding you back?

2.   Remove negativity from the Mind

3.   Understand Happiness and Highest Potential will unfold as it must.

4.   Pursue working on yourself (realize Goal and work on the particulars)

The practice of Yoga is so dynamic however, when you find clarity, you can't stop there, you have to instead go on understanding that clarity interchanges with engaging force which interchanges with being grounded. It is taught that these three forces take forefront at different times.

Yet, through practice you learn how to keep things in their right proportions.

Having a powerful mind comes about when it is most tested. Therefore, to build a strong lifestyle and maintain clarity you have to purify yourself at different times and the way you do this is through what you consume, what you feed your mind, and physical self.

The number one thing that can keep you from achieving the life you want is losing focus on the life you want. So mastery over your mind is crucial in establishing a sound foundation for living a whole healthy life where you are accomplishing the things you want.

Constantly Re-centering the Pendulum

In Yoga, constant re-centering is built upon Abhyasa or (Practice)

Abhyasa is:

How to Change your life

Two Ways to recharge and rebalance yourself is through Breath

The best way to harness energy is through the breath. The energy which flows in comes as (Prana "life force") with breath.

Changing your Life Rapidly but with Time

Intensity and Success:

You must bring a certain level intensity to stay with something, from that you get emotional power to produce intensity.

Intensity:

Emotion Induces State

State Induces Intensity

Intensity Induces Action

Actions Produce Results.

What is Pain?

Is pain the feeling you get when you step on your child's toy when walking to the bathroom, or is it the pain to remember to take out the garbage? Life is a constant reminder of pain, therefore it is important not to lose the battle to the most damaging pain, and that is feeling lost and without in life.

In Yoga:

• Pain is the inability to be in touch with true self.

• Ending Suffering- Is being able to say "I'll never feel pain again."

When you are in good health you are able to encounter pain, anger. And deal with it instead of allowing it to guide you.

So to remove pain you must release that which is hurting you within, make the focus of that thing smaller. Then begin accepting your life to be one without pain. Seek to then get in touch with who you really are and begin to live your life's passions.

Power Building

Body and Longevity = Breathe and Body: Meditation releases stress and cleans the lymphatic system.

Detachment and Vairagya= Body, breath, and mind being able to disassociate pleasure impulse, engaging in focus.

To build power with the things you do, you must seek them often. Meditating and focusing upon self-refinement will help to catalyze growth in all areas of your life. Ever notice when dieting, or changing how and what you consume physically and mentally you gain deeper focus? Well that is due to the ability to "detach" from the things holding you back.

Engaging Empathy Head On

Clarity is being able to understand both your side and what you think is actually the reason "why" they are doing what they are doing. This is called Viveka. Clarity means to See Clearly.

Correct Understanding is called Pramana:

>1.Pratyaksa- Seeing it experientially

>2. Anumana- Inference (Analysis)

>3.Agama- Trust (Faith)

Learning how to understand which ever set of lenses you are using to understand "things" and "people" you can compare your thoughts to the above three areas to review , what your influence may be for the thoughts you are having.

True That

What is true: "With your experience be arriving at what is true" – Dali Lama

Nature of the Universe is to grow so therefore there is no one right way. What is right is constantly changing. There is only sound guidance and choice.

We should be nice to people because people can only function off of three things when acting and making decisions: (Faith) (Tradition) (Reason)

Next time realize that the best choices are made through analyzing how it will limit you or those around you, or enhance the situation. As my grandfather taught me "The good which we do builds our relationship with other humans and nature, and that which is bad destroys the relationship." Acting responsible for your destiny is an art, but acting responsible for your influence on others is a calling. With steady focus you can begin to see how the two are connected.

Suffer No More

To keep from suffering:

1.   Remove it

2.   Don't add to it

3 reasons why we suffer according to Yoga:

Adhyatmika Duhka "Own perceptions"- Suffering due to ourselves.

Adhibhautika- Suffering Do to others doing to us.

Adhidaivika- Natural Typhoons.

Pick the ones you can control and then work to change them! As seen however, natural typhoons do happen in our lives therefore understanding how to see the good in everything is important.

Live you're Dharma: Release the Mind from Unnecessary Stress

"Have a goal but if you focus on process you cannot be versatile"

Tapas – Svadhyaya –isvana-prain-dhana

• Constantly reflecting on past experiences, this is part of living your dharma, don't worry too much about the things you should and should not do, first establish if its good or bad, destructive towards your goal, whether it has heart "meaning" and then do it. Your time after is designed so you can reflect on how it either helped you or harmed you to make the better choice next time.

Consider the lessons- of those who act in the right way. "If I am walking with two other men, each of them will serve as my teacher. I will pick out the good points of the one and imitate them, and the bad points of the other and correct them in myself." – Confucius

Svadharma Dharma is that which protects, holds up and elevates. In the upholding of dharma, every person has a role to play. Each of us, have responsibilities. It is necessary to be clear about what each responsibility entails, and do ones best to live it.

"It is also necessary to be clear about the limits of this responsibility and not to interfere in or worry about things that fall within the orbit of another's responsibility. This is svadharma."

Your life gets messed up when you allow people to influence your choices when you know it's your responsibility to decide. Sometimes you need your dharma to close attention off from the outside and take charge of your life. If people invite you out to a cake factory and your dharma is to go workout. Go workout.

Inspired by Deskichar's teachings: "The moment the attitude is one of na-mama-'not by me', 'not for me', there cannot be any stress."

If you understand yourself and what is meant for your happiness then you can better determine if what you choose has "heart". You can then decide what things do not concern you or what you should worry out. Doing this removes stress.

Working hard towards your goals and getting results is not stressful, it's when you don't see any progress and aren't doing anything anyway just sitting there thinking of the infinite, and all the ways you can fail. That stresses you. Productivity does not stress you.

However, if you are stressed ask yourself these questions:

1.   Do I have faith in what I am doing?

2.   Is what I'm doing meant for me?

3.   Am I tightly married to the cause and desired outcome? Do I crave it enough? Should I create a craving for it?

Goal Chasers

Consider these things when setting out to accomplish your next goal and watch it happen with ease.

1.   Sraddha "compelling reason, tightness" there is then no other option.

2.   Viryam   "Faith"

A lot of times we wait on doing the thing we know we should do to bring us success. Goals are only as powerful as the purpose of it. Goal scoring in soccer is important because it helps you win the game; that reason is attached to the immense pleasure associated with winning, compelling one to want to win.

Fighting Distraction

Things are always going to pop up and distract you, the point isn't to try and avoid them, sometimes you have to stop the car and think could this be a moment the universe wanted me to stop and refocus? That is why reflection is so important but only when done constructively. If you are going to change in life, you can't continually focus on the "old" you, because that is exactly what you will keep producing. Your focus must be in commanding the future you need to believe already exist for you.

Remember these Truths:

"Right Action is the root of all knowledge"

"You are searching for truth –not just desires"

"When man transcends his selfishness, he can begin to see God in other human beings."

"What is, is, what isn't never will be" -Bagvagita

The purpose for Yoga is to have the clarity to do and make the right decision.

When you get married you should let go of things for your spouse.

Sacrifice is:

Sanysa

3 Priorities to uphold, Haruma, Varna: "Calling in life"

1.   Family

2.   Whatever you're calling in life is

3.   Service

In life sometimes you must first misunderstand to understand.

"Every action leaves its residue on you."

Tapas or burn: means discipline on one thing in that moment.

Great things always comes from sacrifice.

Breath places balance in harmony- Stability & Comfort.

Breath brings in stability.

"It's not about fairness to egos but about persevering wholeness"- Mark Orten

Doing the right thing sometimes can be the wrong thing at that time, there is no right way, only a timely way.

Yesterday and today are the same words in Hindi.

Harama- Fixing the mind

Once the mind is full of Swatwa and you have clarity, you will have some knowledge of what to focus on in life. Then you become the master of your senses.

When the mind is distant, the breath is distant. "Where did your breathe go?"

Control the breath and you control the mind.

Yoga removes imbalance, complacency, and tightness, it removes Duhkah and the inability to see things clear or be passionate about something in one's life, or live to one's full potential.

Atman is "I am" energy it gives energy to the mind.

Your personal practice is what matters the most.

Yoga sutra is teaching us to hold onto that which uplifts us and let go that which stops us. At the end of the day you should feel well.

Being positive to things comes with practice.

All the answers come when you have clarity and are not miserable.

A Society with a Problem

Below describes the roots you can find that feed so much discourse in our society. Often, individuals personally lack and feel left out, that is why they seek to destroy the good shining around them. In order to try to create more peace and harmony we must first understand the root of the problem.

Personification of the Tree:

1.   The leaves and branches are Raga- Dvesa, Abhinivesa, = Hatred, Anger, Fear of future

2.   Trunk, Asmita, Ego, Inferiority, insignificance, (Leads to suffering)

3.   Roots- Avdya= Ignorance, or wrong

Solution:

Avidya x Vidya = Get to know / Correct your knowledge

Asmita x Vinaya= Accept your strength & Weakness

Praga Dvesa x Vairayga = Detachment, Grounded, you know where you are and should be.

Abhinivesa x Isvara Pranishava: Surrender into a higher force. Faith= No Fear

Viveka – Wisdom to know where you stand and be ok with it, or seek to change it.

By the Grace of God

The grace of God is what empowers you to live an uncommon life. The grace of God will continue to show you and teach you about the bad things you do, yet you will never be condemned by God! Remember the enemy does not want you to know you already have won! So in everything you do rejoice in your positive outcome.

Ready to Practice some Yoga?

"Failure is a perceived reality, so too is achievement, make a choice in what to focus on because when it is dark enough, you can see the stars." – Christopher Cole

Ultimately Lead with your Heart & Mind

So now that I have shared my heart with you, I hope truly that you have been able to journey through my writings to a place where there is no discouragement, only courage. I want for you to understand with crisp clarity that anything is possible for your life, and to value the reality that your actions matter in influencing greater love and happiness in this world. I challenge you to listen more to your heart's calling for your feelings and direction and your mind for your thoughts to influence your actions to be the very best they can be for your current life.

A powerful book written on Leadership titled *True North* taught that great leaders who add tremendous value and authenticity to this world are those who lead with their hearts and their minds. From each Mindfullesson I know that it can help guide you towards the very best. Experience love and happiness now and keep it forever.

"If it doesn't go through the heart before the mind it is not divine."

-Christopher Cole

Made in the USA
San Bernardino, CA
15 April 2015